12.99

SEASONS

By Melvin Berger
Illustrated by Ron Jones

DOUBLEDAY
NEW YORK LONDON TORONTO SYDNEY AUCKLAND

SEASONS

Published by Doubleday, a division of
Bantam Doubleday Dell Publishing
Group, Inc.
666 Fifth Avenue,
New York, New York 10103

Doubleday and the portrayal of an anchor
with a dolphin are trademarks of
Doubleday, a division of Bantam Doubleday
Dell Publishing Group, Inc.

Library of Congress Cataloging-in-
Publication Data

Berger, Melvin.
    Seasons/Melvin Berger.
    p. cm.
    Includes index.
    Summary: Describes, in simple text and
illustrations, the seasons and the effect they
have on the earth.
    1. Seasons—Juvenile literature.
[1. Seasons.] I. Title. QB637.4.B47 1990
508—dc20   89-32126   CIP   AC

ISBN 0-385-24876-8
ISBN 0-385-24877-6 (lib. bdg.)
R. L. 3.3

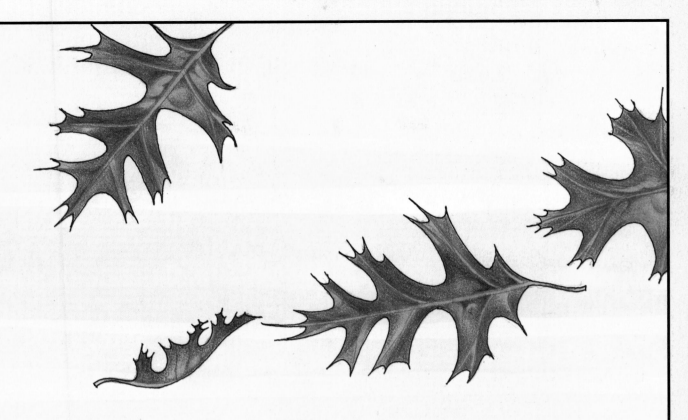

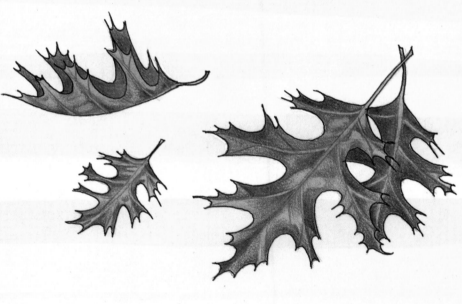

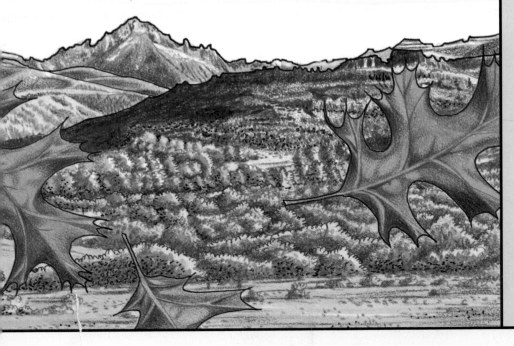

Introduction

Did you ever wonder why . . .
- the weather is sometimes warm and sometimes cold?
- the days are sometimes long and sometimes short?
- plants grow and die and then grow again?
- animals show up at certain times and disappear at other times?

These changes occur because the year is divided into periods we call seasons. The seasons—spring, summer, autumn, winter—are as old as the earth itself.

To early humans, changes in nature must have seemed very frightening. In autumn they saw leaves falling from trees and worried that new leaves would never grow again. In winter they saw lakes freezing over and feared the ice would never melt. In the spring they were surprised by the sudden appearance of many different kinds of birds and animals. And in the hot, dry summer, they despaired that the rain and cool weather were gone for all time.

The mysterious changes led primitive people to try to control nature. At the end of summer, people covered their bodies with leaves and flowers and did special dances to try to hold back the cold weather. When spring finally returned, they chanted prayers and made offerings of thanksgiving.

A few of these ancient rites have continued down to our own times. Just before Easter in some German villages, the young people still make a straw man and dress it in leather pants and a fur cap. Then they raise him on a pole and march through the streets, singing songs about carrying Death away and bringing in May flowers.

From time to time, the marchers stop to dance around the straw man, loudly whooping and shouting. When they reach a certain field, they tear apart the straw man, break the wooden pole into pieces, and set everything on fire. Then the villagers dance around the blaze to celebrate spring's victory over winter.

The ancient Greeks made up stories to explain the passing of the seasons. One such legend tells of Demeter, goddess of the earth and agriculture, and Persephone, her beautiful daughter. Once, while Persephone was gathering flowers in a meadow, the earth opened up in front of her. Hades, god of the underworld, appeared, seized the terrified girl, and carried her off to his kingdom deep inside the earth.

Demeter was grief-stricken. She searched everywhere but could find no trace of Persephone. Finally, though, the Sun told Demeter that Persephone was being held against her will in the lower world.

Demeter became so sad that she no longer cared for the plants on earth. They all withered and died. Nothing new would grow. There was famine in the land.

The other gods begged Demeter to end

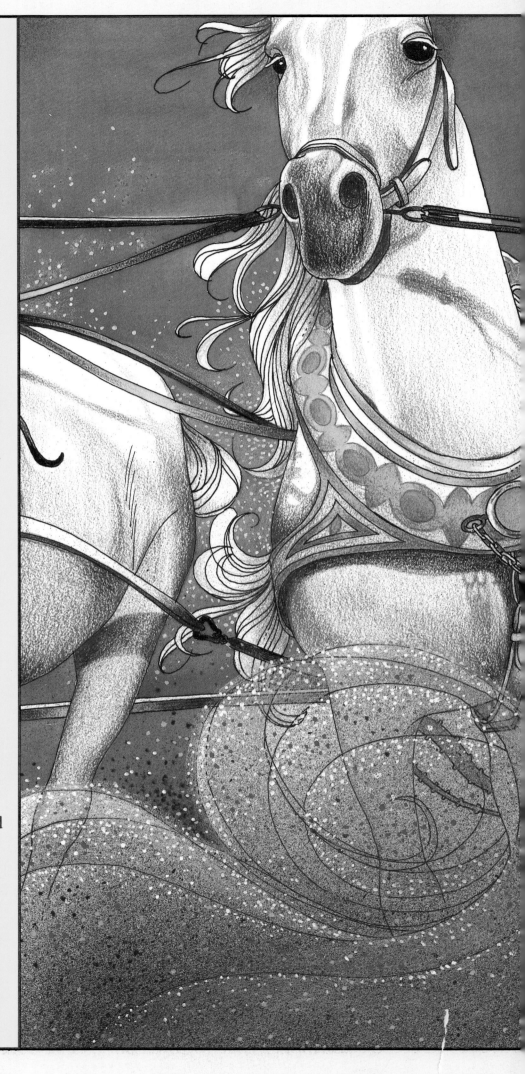

her grieving. She refused. The earth would bear no fruit, she said, until she saw her daughter again. The gods then appealed to Zeus, king of the gods, who agreed to rescue Persephone.

Meanwhile the beautiful Persephone had been refusing to take any food. She knew that eating anything in the lower world would mean that she could never leave there.

But Hades was very clever. He sent his servants to earth to bring back the most tempting morsels that could be found. They returned with the seeds of a pomegranate fruit. Hades then told Persephone that seeds are not really food and she ate one.

When the all-powerful Zeus sent his golden coach to the underworld, he was able to bring Persephone back to Demeter. But then Zeus learned that Persephone had tasted the seed while with Hades. The mighty god became very angry and issued the following command: Persephone would have to go down to the world of the dead for six months of every year. For the rest of the time, though, she could live with her mother.

According to the Greeks, this is how the changing seasons became part of our natural world. While Persephone is in the underworld, Demeter does not let anything grow. It is winter on earth. Then Persephone returns to her mother and Demeter makes the earth come alive. It is springtime. At the end of summer, Persephone returns to the underworld and the long winter begins again. The world remains cold and dark until Persephone comes back again, bringing another spring.

Today we follow a few magical practices and retell the old stories about the seasons. But unlike the people of long ago, we know how and why the seasons change. Much of the mystery is gone but not the joy and wonder the seasons bring!

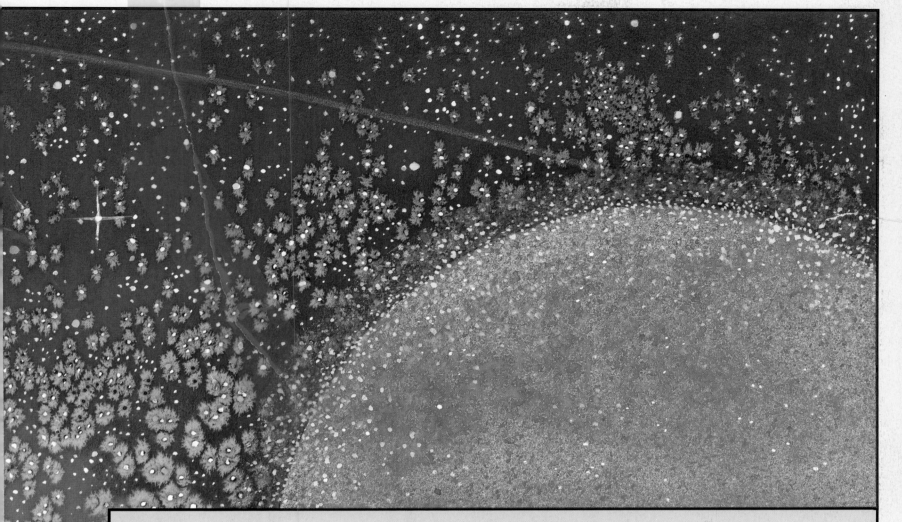

What Makes the Seasons?

Everyone knows the four seasons:

- Spring—from about March 21 to June 21. The weather gets milder and warmer, the days become longer, and plants begin to grow again.
- Summer—from about June 21 to September 22, the hottest season. The temperature is high, the days are long, and most plants are in full bloom.
- Autumn—from about September 22 to December 21. The temperature drops, the days grow shorter, and many fruits and vegetables are harvested.
- Winter—from about December 21 to March 21. The coldest season, with lots of snow in many places, short days and long nights, and almost no plant growth in the northern areas.

But do you know what *makes* the seasons?

The seasons change because of the tilt of the earth.

Think of an imaginary line, called an axis, passing straight through planet earth from top to bottom. The top end of the make-believe axis is the North Pole. The bottom end is the South Pole. The earth spins around, or rotates, on this north-south axis. It takes twenty-four hours, or one day, to make one complete rotation.

The earth's axis, though, is not straight up and down in relation to the sun. The axis tips slightly at an angle of about 23.5 degrees.

At the same time the earth rotates around its axis, it also loops around the sun in a great, sweeping orbit. It takes one year, 365 days, for the earth to complete this orbit.

Throughout the earth's year-long trip around the sun, the tilt stays the same.

That means that for part of its journey the North Pole is tipped toward the sun. For another part it is tipped away. And in between it is not tipped toward or away from the sun.

When the North Pole is tilted toward the sun, the sun's rays are focused directly on the northern half of the earth. The weather is warm, and there are more hours of sunlight and fewer hours of darkness. It is summer in the part of earth we call the Northern Hemisphere.

When the North Pole is tilted away from the sun, the sun's rays are spread out over a larger area. Since the sun's rays now cover more space, they give less heat to each point they reach. The weather is cold and there are fewer hours of daylight and longer nights. It is winter in the Northern Hemisphere.

When earth is moving from summer to winter or from winter to summer, the tilt is neither toward the sun nor away. Without the tilt, the weather is neither hot nor cold. Days and nights are about equal in length. Between summer and winter comes autumn; between winter and summer it is spring.

Would you like to see how the seasons change? You'll need a small lamp for the sun and a globe of the earth.

First check to see whether your globe is tilted like planet earth. If not, hold it tipped to one side.

Next find where you live on the globe and mark the spot with a chalk "X" or a removable sticker.

Now in a dark room hold the globe with the North Pole leaning toward the lamp, or

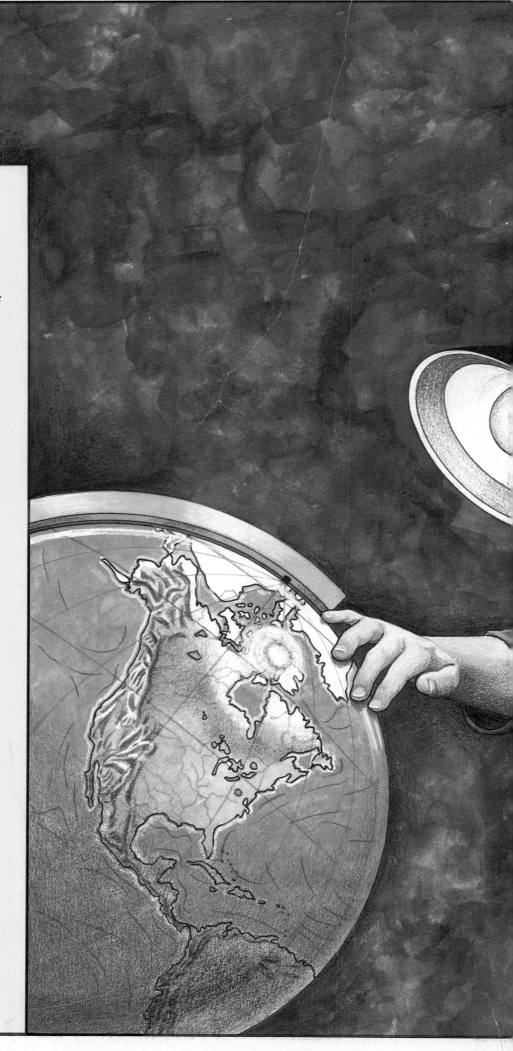

sun. The bright light falling on the top half of the globe is like summer in the Northern Hemisphere. If you live in the United States, you would be enjoying nice warm weather.

Slowly rotate the globe one complete turn. See how the place where you live spends more time in the light. That means the days are longer than the nights.

Keeping the tilt of the globe the same, walk in a circle halfway around toward the other side of the lamp. Now the light shining on the globe is not as bright. Therefore it is not as hot. It is autumn. When you rotate the globe, you'll see that your spot spends equal time in the light and in the dark.

Without changing the tilt, continue walking until you're opposite your starting point. The North Pole should now be slanting away from the light. This is the Northern Hemisphere at the winter tilt. Because the light is less direct, the weather is cold. Rotate the globe through a whole day and see how your spot spends less time in the light and more in the dark. Less daylight means shorter days and longer nights.

Finally, walk halfway back to your starting point. The light is the same as it was in autumn. The temperature is moderate and the hours of daylight and darkness are the same. It is spring.

You can notice these seasonal changes if you live in the United States or any other country in the so-called Temperate Zone. But things are very different at the North Pole and the Frigid Zone north of the Arctic Circle.

Try this. Hold your globe at the winter tilt—North Pole away from the sun—and rotate it through a whole day. Do you see how the pole stays in the dark all the time? In the winter it is dark at the North Pole twenty-four hours a day.

Now hold the globe at the summer tilt. Rotate it through a whole day. See how the light strikes the North Pole the entire time. During the summer the sun shines on the North Pole day and night. That is why the far north is sometimes called the Land of the Midnight Sun.

Halfway between the poles on your globe is an imaginary circle. It forms a ring around the earth called the equator. Keeping the globe at the summer tilt, watch one point on the equator as you rotate the globe. Do you see how the point spends equal time in the light and in the dark? If you also rotate the globe at the winter tilt, you'll discover that day and night are the same all year long.

The lands around the equator are hot all the time. This is called the Tropical Zone. The Tropical Zone extends from the Tropic of Cancer north of the equator to the Tropic of Capricorn south of the equator.

The weather changes very little from one season to the next in the Tropical Zone.

The biggest difference through the year is the amount of rain. Most countries close to the equator have one wet season, with lots of rain. Then it is dry for the rest of the year. The wet and dry seasons depend on the wind patterns in that area. Some tropical lands, though, are deserts. They barely get any rain all year long.

People who live in the Northern Hemisphere sometimes forget what the seasons are like on the other side of the equator. When the North Pole is tilted toward the sun, the South Pole is tilted away. And when the North Pole is tilted away from the sun, the South Pole is tilted in the sun's direction.

Since the tilt makes the seasons, an opposite tilt in the Southern Hemisphere reverses the seasons. When it's summer in the Northern Hemisphere, it's winter in the Southern Hemisphere. And when it's winter in the north, it's summer in the south.

If you live in the United States and are too hot next summer, you can hop a plane and cool off in Argentina, where it is winter. And if you live in Australia and grow tired of swimming in December, you can fly to Germany and spend Christmas playing in the snow!

Spring

At first you don't notice it. The temperature rises just a few degrees from one week to the next. Every day has only a couple more minutes of light than the day before. The angle of sunlight shifts a tiny bit.

Then, suddenly, it's March 21. Spring is here! The sun rises directly in the east and sets directly in the west. It is the date of the vernal equinox. Equinox means "equal night." At the time of the equinox, both day and night are exactly twelve hours long.

As winter ends and spring begins, the sun's rays heat the cold air. This causes winds to blow. At first the winds are cold and blustery. But they soon give way to gentle breezes. The shifting winds also bring more rain. As people slosh through the puddles, they think to themselves, "April showers bring May flowers," and feel happier.

You may not notice day-to-day differences in the spring weather. But you can be sure the plants know that spring is here. The longer days and warmer temperatures bring many wonderful changes. The grass turns green. Fuzzy buds appear on pussy willow branches. Fresh yellow blooms pop out on forsythia bushes. In warmer areas, magnolias bear large white or pink flowers. Tulip, daffodil, and narcissus bulbs push up green shoots that soon blossom into brightly colored flowers.

In the early spring the sap starts to run in the trees. That is when the Indians used to move from their winter villages into the maple forests. They made cuts in the trees and hung buckets to catch the dripping sap. The Indians then boiled the liquid in huge kettles to produce the maple syrup and sugar they used to sweeten their food. Today sap is still gathered and made into syrup in much the same way.

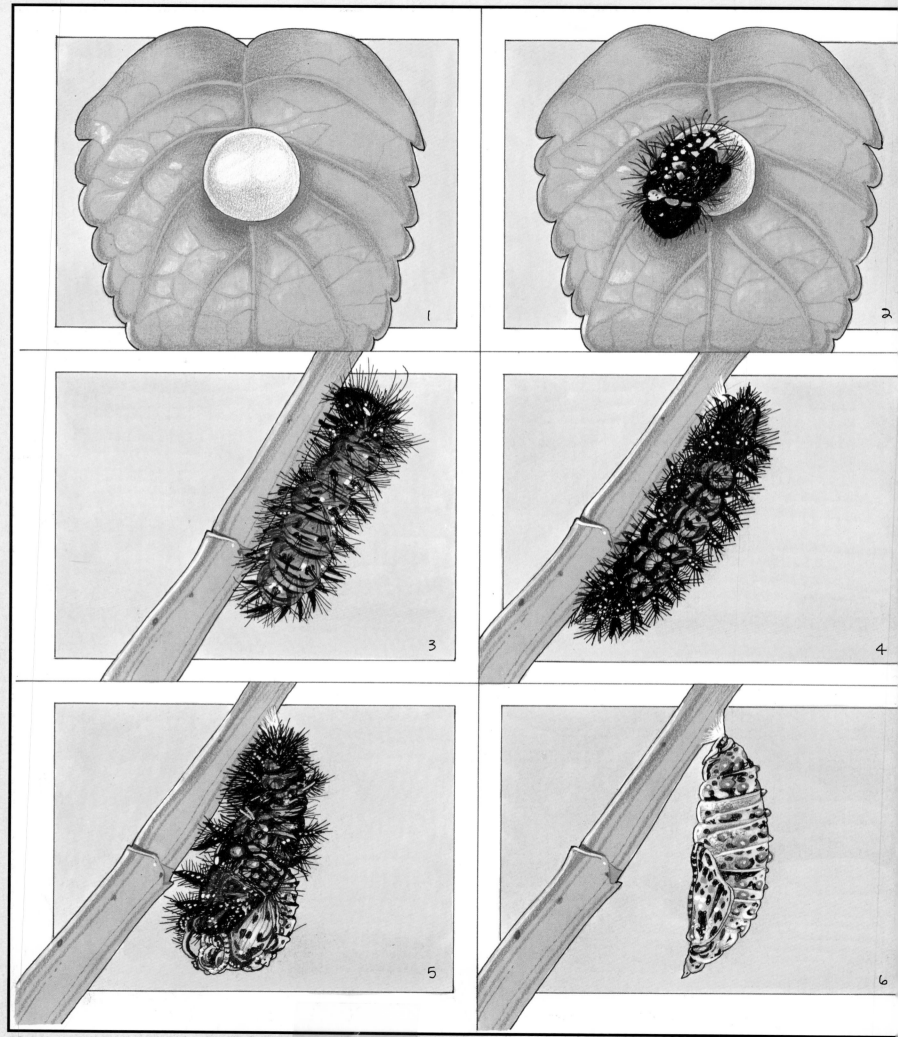

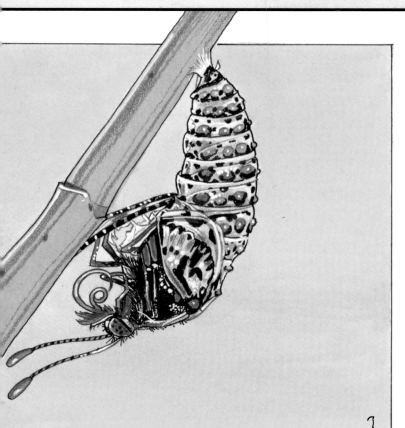

At the beginning of spring, the bare branches of the trees look dead. But they're not dead at all. If you look closely, you'll see that the branches are covered with tiny buds that were formed the summer before.

The buds were on the tree all winter. Now that it is spring, the buds come to life. The outer coverings drop off. The crumpled leaves that were inside open up and turn green. Soon these fresh, new leaves completely cover the tree.

The increased heat and extra light of spring stir the insects into action. The butterfly, for example, starts life as an egg. A few days after the egg is laid, it hatches. Out comes a larva, or caterpillar.

After three weeks or so, the caterpillar spins a "button" of silk on a twig or leaf. The caterpillar's skin splits open and a wiggly, wormlike creature, called a pupa, works its way out. The pupa grabs the silk button and holds on while a hard shell, called a chrysalis, forms around it.

About two weeks go by. The chrysalis just hangs in one place, not moving or changing. But inside it the most extraordinary things are happening. The pupa is becoming a butterfly!

Soon the butterfly is ready to break loose from the chrysalis. It pushes out its legs, crawls out, and opens up its soft, wet wings. In a few minutes the wings are dry and firm. And off flies the butterfly in search of food and a mate.

Meanwhile huge numbers of birds are flying north from their winter homes in the south. They build nests of every size—from the ruby-throated hummingbird's tiny nest of green lichen and cobwebs to the osprey's nest of tree limbs up to two feet long. Then they lay their eggs in the nest and sit on them for two or three weeks until they hatch.

The mating flights of male and female mallard ducks are fun to watch. The birds dive into the water, come up with their wings spread, and perform acrobatic tricks in the air. After mating, they fill their nests with as many as twelve or fifteen eggs. Right after the eggs hatch, the newborn ducklings are able to walk. The mother leads them off in search of food.

The longer hours of sunlight and warmer temperatures signal the whales and herring that it's time to head north. Other sea creatures also get ready to mate and lay eggs. Certain fish like the salmon may take several months to swim the long distances from the ocean to the rivers and streams where they will bear their young.

Bats, bears, woodchucks, and chipmunks have been asleep most of the winter. When they wake up in the spring, they set out to find their first meal. People who live in the country may see brown bats swooping and flitting through the evening sky, scooping up as many bugs as they can find. Bats eat as much as half their weight every night!

Like many other animals, raccoons mate in the early spring. The mother bears two to seven soft, furry little creatures in late April or May. The babies are blind at birth and weigh about as much as a small bar of soap. But after only two months the young raccoons are ready to leave their tree home. They follow their mother down the tree trunk and join her in digging in the earth for worms, searching fallen logs for grubs, and, of course, overturning garbage cans looking for scraps of food.

Spring is planting time for the farmers. They plow their fields, add fertilizer to the soil, and drop the seeds into the ground in long, straight lines. With the warm air and the moisture in the soil, the seeds soon grow into full-sized plants.

People have found many ways to celebrate the arrival of spring. *Shumbun-no-hi* is the spring holiday in Japan. On that day people visit the family cemetery. Instead of mourning, though, they think happy thoughts about those who have passed away. The occasion usually includes a picnic-type meal at the cemetery.

April Fools' Day comes on April 1. It is a time to play harmless pranks and tricks on friends. The custom began in France about four hundred years ago when that country made January 1 the start of the year instead of April 1. Some people, though, kept on observing New Year's Day on April 1. They were called April fools and were given silly presents, such as a bouquet of onion plants instead of flowers.

The English celebrate May 1 with dances around tall Maypoles, much like the springtime worship of trees long, long ago. Each dancer holds the end of a long, gaily colored ribbon that is attached to the top of the pole. As the dancers move around the pole, they weave the ribbons into a beautiful design.

Many religions have spring celebrations that have both seasonal *and* historical meanings. Jews, for example, mark the spring season with three holidays—*Tu b'Shevat,* Purim, and Passover. *Tu b'Shevat* is a sort of birthday party for trees. On that day Jews celebrate by eating the fruit of trees native to Israel, such as dates, nuts, and figs, and by staying up most of the night studying the Bible.

The feast of Purim marks the rescue of the Jews from slaughter by the Persians in 600 B.C. Although the holiday celebrates a historical event, it still resembles other folk holidays of the spring season.

During the Jewish festival of Passover, the entire family eats a traditional meal known as the seder. The seder plate contains six symbols of the occasion. Among them are parsley and a roasted egg. The parsley stands for the return of green plants in the spring. The roasted egg, which reminds guests of the burnt offerings the Jews used to bring to temple, also represents the new life that returns to nature around Passover time.

For Christians Easter is the most important spring holiday. It is based on the death and resurrection, or rising from the dead, of Jesus Christ. At the same time it commemorates nature's awakening and rebirth.

Easter does not have a fixed date. It is the first Sunday after the first full moon on or after March 21. Therefore Easter can come on any Sunday between March 22 and April 25.

Many children believe that an Easter bunny brings their Easter eggs. This belief may have come from ancient lands where people considered the rabbit a symbol of the moon. The rabbit may have become associated with Easter because the moon determines the start of Easter.

The custom of coloring eggs for Easter also started very long ago. In some countries people colored eggs red to symbolize the joy of the resurrection. Children today may make baskets and fill them with eggs of many colors.

Candles and blazing bonfires are customary in Easter celebrations. The flames are a reminder that after darkness comes light, after death comes new life.

An impressive fire ceremony takes place in Jerusalem every year on Holy Thursday, three days before Easter Sunday. Fifty churchmen carrying banners and singing march around the tomb of Christ in the Church of the Holy Sepulcher. Then they light a fire with the flames shooting out through openings in the church wall. Thousands of people light their candles at the openings. When everyone enters the church, it glows brightly with all the candlelight, to represent the birth of Christ.

On the morning of Easter Sunday, Christians all over the world go to church. Afterward family and friends get together for Easter dinner. The main dish is usually ham, turkey, or lamb.

How do you celebrate spring? With flowers? Special foods? Worship? Fun and games? No matter. It's sure to have something to do with the wonderful changes that spring brings.

Summer

Today is June 21, the start of summer. It is the day of the summer solstice—the longest day of the year. This solstice comes when the earth's axis tilts most toward the sun. Starting tomorrow there are fewer and fewer hours of sunlight every day.

July is the first full month of summer. It is also the hottest month of the year. People sometimes call the uncomfortable days of July the "dog days." That's because Sirius, the so-called Dog Star, can be seen every night from early July until mid-August. But Sirius has nothing to do with the hot weather. It just happens to be visible in the sky at this time.

Thunderstorms often break out on summer afternoons. All morning the blazing sun warms the water in oceans and lakes. More and more water evaporates and becomes water vapor in the air.

The water vapor forms into tiny droplets of water. They come together in big, dark clouds. Soon it starts to rain, harder and harder. Then, all of a sudden, a bolt of lightning zigzags across the sky. Moments later a roar of thunder shakes the ground.

The lightning occurs because the clouds get a powerful electrical charge during a storm. The clouds contain both large and small droplets of water. The large droplets have a positive electrical charge. The smaller ones have a negative charge. The two different kinds of charges build up the electricity in the cloud until a giant spark leaps between the cloud and the earth.

As the lightning flashes through the sky, it heats the air around it. The hot air expands in all directions, producing the roaring sound of the thunder.

Sometimes a rainbow appears when the sun shines after a rain shower. Sunlight contains all the colors of the rainbow—red, orange, yellow, green, blue, indigo, and violet. As the light passes through the tiny rain drops still in the air, the rays of light are bent. When this happens, the sunlight separates out into its different colors.

Do you see how one end of the rainbow seems to rest on the earth? According to an old legend, if you find the end of the rainbow, you'll find a pot of gold there! Sad to say, it is only a legend. No one has ever found the end of the rainbow—or the pot of gold.

Many flowers thrive in the heat of summer. Roses, daisies, zinnias, snapdragons, and other blossoms brighten gardens and roadsides. Wherever they grow, all flowers have the same basic parts: petals, sepals, stamens, and pistils.

The petals are the most colorful part of the flower. It is the petals that attract the insects. The curly green leaves at the flower's base are the sepals. The long, thin stamens are the male part of the flower; their tips are covered with tiny grains of pollen. Standing upright at the center ready to receive the pollen is the pistil, the female part of the flower.

Bees and other insects flit from flower to flower, carrying pollen from stamens to pistils. The wind also transfers the pollen within one flower or from one flower to another. When pollen lands on the sticky pistil, seeds for new plants begin to form.

The animals that were born during the spring grow quickly during the summer. Young birds learn to fly. No one is quite sure exactly how this happens. Some think that the parent holds food just out of reach of the little bird. The bird has to stretch to

STAMEN

POLLEN

PISTIL

SEPAL

PETAL

get the food. Each time the parent holds the food a little farther away. Finally the young bird hops over the edge of the nest, flaps its wings, and flies toward the food.

All summer long, birds keep searching for things to eat. Swallows and warblers flutter about, catching insects. Woodpeckers dig for insects in tree trunks. Robins and woodcocks pull worms out of the ground. Cardinals peck at plants that have the seeds they like. Eagles, owls, and hawks spot the rats and mice they want for dinner. And gulls and herons dip and dive along shorelines in search of their seafood meals.

Summer is the season for insects—and lots of them! The hotter the day, the more the bugs hum, buzz, flit, flutter, creep, and crawl around. Because they grow and multiply so fast, several generations of insects can be born in a single summer.

Take the common—and pesty—housefly as an example. The female housefly lays eggs perhaps four times a year. And she lays up to 250 eggs at a time. That means that one fly can give birth to as many as one thousand flies a year!

Each fly egg looks like a yellowish grain of rice. After about a day the egg hatches. It becomes a larva, a tiny, wormlike creature that is often called a maggot. Several days later the larva forms an oval case around itself. At this stage it is a pupa. Finally, in about four or five days, an adult fly wriggles out of the case.

A hornets' nest on a hot summer day is a busy place. The nest, which is about as large as your head, houses more than two thousand white-faced insects. Like a fly, the hornet can see in all directions. Its eyes are made up of hundreds of separate lenses. Facing every which way, these lenses give hornets a very wide range of vision.

Although hornets prefer the nectar from flowers, they also eat other insects. Each victim they catch is brought back to the nest to feed the newborn hornets.

Listen on any hot summer afternoon or evening, especially in the country, and you'll hear crickets. Although you seldom see one, you know they're around. The loud katydids, which look like green, hunchbacked grasshoppers, come out in late summer. Many katydids start their sound at twilight and keep it up all night long. Tradition says the first frost will arrive six weeks after the first katydid is heard.

While most animals are very active during the summer, others take a long summer nap called estivation. Many lizards and rodents that live in the desert estivate. While they're asleep they need almost no water. This is fortunate, because water is in very short supply during the hot summer months.

One of the more amazing beings to enjoy a snooze during the dry summer season is the lungfish. Found in Africa, Australia, and South America, the lungfish can breathe in the air as well as underwater. During the summer the lungfish builds a mud shell around itself. It lives on the air inside the shell and the fat in its body. With the next rainy season, the mud softens and out swims the well-rested lungfish.

Other animals have their own ways of dealing with the heat and dryness of summer. Panting helps keep dogs cool, even when the temperature is in the

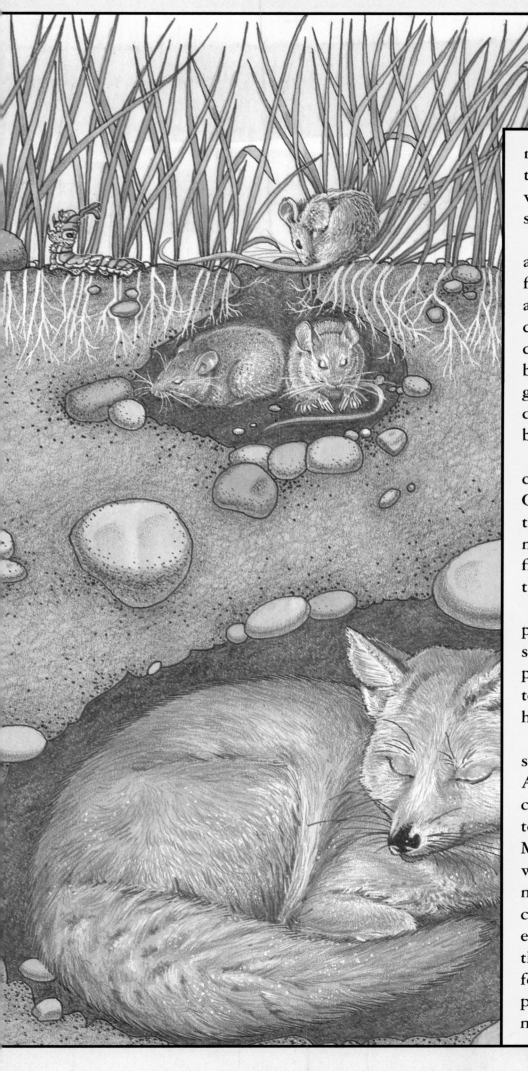

nineties. Hares and rabbits lose heat through the skin of their big ears. And on very hot days foxes, mice, and jack rabbits stay underground to keep cool.

In the Middle Ages, Midsummer Eve, around the night of June 21, was a most fearful time. People believed that witches and evil fairies got new powers with the coming of the summer solstice. The wicked creatures were thought to fly about on broomsticks or ride through the air on giant black cats. To frighten away the demon spirits, the ancient people lit huge bonfires on hilltops.

In some places, Midsummer Eve ceremonies continue to this day. People in Cornwall, England, light a chain of fires that blazes out from hill to hill for many miles. The villagers dance around these fires, keeping their backs to the light and their faces toward the dark.

When the flames die down, the young people take hands and jump over the smoldering embers for good luck. In the past farmers drove cattle across the embers to cure them of disease or to keep them healthy.

As the summer goes on, the days grow shorter and the nights longer. On late August evenings there is sometimes a little chill in the air. And by September it's easy to tell that summer is coming to an end. More and more birds are flying off to warmer climates. The last generation of monarch butterflies emerges from its cocoons. Tall stalks of goldenrod bloom everywhere. In the fields the farmers cut the golden-colored grass to make hay to feed their animals. And kids everywhere put away their swim suits and baseball mitts and head back to school.

Autumn

Autumn begins at the autumnal equinox, which arrives on either September 22 or 23. There are exactly twelve hours between sunrise and sunset and between sunset and sunrise. But starting now the days shrink, the nights get longer, and the temperature drops until winter.

The most striking feature of autumn in temperate zones is the changing color of the tree leaves. During the summer months each leaf was really a food factory. The raw materials were water that came up from the roots and the air all around. The energy came from the sunlight. And to help it all work there was a green substance in the leaf called chlorophyll. The food produced by the leaves allowed the tree to grow bigger and taller.

But with the coming of autumn the food factories in the leaves start to shut down. The bright green color of the chlorophyll fades. The colors that had been in the leaf all along—yellow, red, orange, and purple—but were hidden by the chlorophyll, can now be seen.

The exact colors you see in the autumn leaves depend on the amount of each color in the different kinds of trees. Maple leaves become red and orange. Birches show a brilliant yellow. And oak and dogwood turn deep red or purple.

The leaves then drop from the trees, giving the season its other name, "fall." The fallen leaves pile up on the ground. Walking through them is like stepping through giant bowls of cornflakes! People rake the leaves around their homes. But what happens to the leaves people don't sweep away?

Birds and worms nibble on the leaves. At the same time, germs, rain, and the weight of the leaves changes them into a soft mass called leaf mold. In time the mold becomes dark, rich soil in which other plants can grow.

By autumn most trees and plants have produced seeds. The seeds last through the whole winter. The following spring, when the soil is warm and moist, the seeds will sprout and new trees and plants will begin to grow.

Some seeds like the coconut are immense. Others, like the dozens of seeds found in every strawberry, are tiny. And somewhere in between are the pits of such fruits as apples, oranges, and pears.

Nature has thousands of clever ways to scatter tree and plant seeds. The winglike seeds of the maple and ash trees are carried great distances by the wind. The smooth pods of the honey locust tree skate across the ground. Dandelion seeds float through the air on fluffy parachutes. Several kinds of seeds have hooks that catch on the fur of animals and later fall onto the soil. Squirrels collect and bury many nuts and acorns, which are really seeds. And birds eat grapes and berries and drop the seeds wherever they fly.

But what of plants like the daisy that don't make seeds during the summer? How do they survive?

Even though their flowers die, the roots of many "seedless" plants stay alive underground all winter. And the roots start to grow again the following spring.

Tulips, daffodils, onions, and other plants survive because they have special thick stems called bulbs. If you peel apart

the bulb of an onion—though it'll make you cry—you'll see many separate layers packed full of food for the future plant. You'll also find a central white bud from which the leaves will grow in the spring.

Some flowers, such as chrysanthemums, asters, and gentians, only bloom in the autumn. Scientists call these "short-day" plants. They only flower in the autumn, when there are no more than twelve or thirteen hours of sunlight, instead of the fourteen or more hours during summer.

Come autumn, most insects seem to vanish. Many die when the weather gets cold. But they leave behind tremendous numbers of immature, unborn insects, called larvae and pupae. In this state they survive the winter and develop into adult insects in the spring.

Grasshoppers, locusts, and katydids also lay their eggs in the autumn ground—and die. The following spring the eggs hatch. As the newborns eat, they grow large and shed their skins several times. Eventually they grow wings and fly away.

Many birds, including robins, bluebirds, house wrens, red-winged blackbirds, Baltimore orioles, and most wild ducks and geese head south, or migrate, with the coming of autumn. How do birds know it is time to fly away—even before the ground freezes and their food disappears? Probably they see or sense that the days are getting shorter. The fewer hours of sunshine tell them it's time to travel.

Most migrating birds travel very long distances. But the arctic tern holds the record. After spending the summer near the Arctic Circle, it flies 22,000 miles south to Antarctica in the autumn!

Scientists are still not sure how birds are able to find their way on these long migrations. Some birds fly at night or over the sea. Perhaps they use the stars to guide them. Or maybe it's something in the wind or the sun's path across the sky that sends them to the same exact spot year after year.

But not all birds migrate. Cardinals, bobwhites, and many others tend to stay north all year long. They get ready for the rough weather ahead by growing soft, downy feathers next to their skins. Like a down-lined jacket, the little fluffy feathers trap the body heat and keep the birds warm.

Just before winter many animals go on an eating binge. Woodchucks stuff themselves with huge amounts of clover and alfalfa. Raccoons devour everything from garbage to bird eggs. Field mice consume huge numbers of seeds. Squirrels fill their mouths and cheeks with nuts and acorns and hide them for later. Foxes feast on as many rabbits, snakes, and rats as they can catch. And chipmunks gobble up whatever they can find.

All this overeating gives these animals lots of extra fat. During the coming winter months, when it is cold and hard to find food, this fat will supply them with both heat and energy.

Except for those who live in climates that are always warm, humans must also prepare for winter in autumn. Farmers harvest their crops. Homeowners make sure that the woodpile is stacked and the oil tank full. Families shop for new supplies of sweaters, boots, gloves, and wool socks. Heavy blankets come out of the closet, along with jackets and long coats.

The first frost usually comes around late October in the more northern areas.

Afterward there is almost always a week or more of warm days and clear nights. This time is called Indian Summer.

Indian Summer probably got its name from the Native Americans who told the early settlers to expect this spell of warm weather. It is caused by a mass of warm, dry air staying in place over a large section of the country.

Around the time of Indian Summer, people start thinking about Halloween, pumpkins, and trick-or-treating. This popular autumn holiday began with the ancient Celts. They believed that on the night of October 31 ghosts, witches, elves, and fairies came out to harm people. Cats were also to be feared on that night, since it was said that evil human beings were changed into cats.

Many centuries later, in the year 835 A.D., the Christian Church took over the Celt festival, calling it either All Saints' Day or All Hallows' Day. The night before was named All Hallows' Eve and then shortened to Halloween. By now Halloween has become a holiday for all people. But it is still connected to ghosts, witches, and scary black cats!

The fourth Thursday of November is Thanksgiving. It is a national holiday to give thanks for a good harvest. The custom probably grew out of old English harvest celebrations. On Thanksgiving Day people like to gather together for big family parties and to enjoy delicious turkey dinners.

By the middle of December the trees are bare, the flowers have withered, most insects are dead, and the migrating birds have flown south.

Autumn is nearly over. Winter is coming in.

Winter

Today is the shortest day of the year. In the north chilling winds blow over freshly fallen snow. The streets and roads are slick with ice. The temperature is in the frigid twenties. But it feels even colder because of the howling winds. The date is December 21, the start of winter and the day of the winter solstice.

After today the days start to grow longer, with about two minutes of extra sunlight every day. But it still stays very cold. As the old saying goes, "The day lengthens, the cold strengthens." January is actually the coldest month of the year.

Snowstorms are a familiar part of northern winters. When violent winds and intense cold come with the snow, we get a blizzard. Huge drifts of snow pile up, roads get blocked, electric power lines fall, airplanes stop flying, and schools close

their doors. Most everything stops until the blizzard ends and the snow is cleared away.

Of course, the farther south you go, the milder the winters. In Florida, for example, the average temperature in January is about 56 degrees Fahrenheit. Should there be a cold spell and a snowfall, the flakes usually melt as soon as they touch the ground, which is warmer than the air. Occasional frosts, though, can damage the oranges and other crops that grow in the south.

All winter long tree and plant seeds lie in or on the ground, protected by their heavy outer shells. But each freezing and thawing breaks open the outer shell a little bit. Water seeps into the opening. By the time spring arrives, the seed is ready to sprout and grow.

While some animals stay busy all winter, others just go to sleep. They hibernate. Among the animals that hibernate are bats and squirrels, snakes and chipmunks, turtles and woodchucks.

Bears generally spend most of the winter asleep. But they do not truly hibernate. From time to time they wake up and walk around. Black and brown bears sleep in caves or in uprooted tree roots. Female polar bears mostly snuggle in ice caves or dens dug in the snow. Strangely enough male polar bears do not seem to sleep at all!

Woodchucks (also called groundhogs) dig down into a burrow, or hole in the ground. They seal the entrance with dirt, huddle together, and go to sleep. Hardly breathing at all, they wait out the winter.

According to an old legend, if a groundhog comes out of its hole on February 2 and sees its shadow, there will be six more weeks of winter. If there is no shadow, then winter is over and spring is about to arrive.

In the town of Punxsutawney, Pennsylvania, the Groundhog Club has

been watching many generations of local groundhogs every February since 1898. Unfortunately the little critters have been wrong as many times as they have been right!

Mink, ermine, beaver, fox, and other animals do not hibernate. Instead they grow thick new coats of fur in early winter. This protects them against the cold weather. Sometimes the winter fur is white in color and acts as camouflage for animals that live in snowy areas.

Like all living creatures, you and I must keep warm in cold weather. Partly we do this by eating food. Our body changes the food into heat energy, which helps to keep us warm. And we keep warm by wearing proper clothing. Did you know, for example, that more than fifty percent of your body heat is lost through your head? A wool sock hat and a scarf on really cold days helps to cut this heat loss.

Feet are also chilled by cold, wet, or icy ground. Two pairs of socks—a snug-fitting nylon pair underneath and a heavy, woolen pair on top—will help keep your toes toasty warm.

People can stay warm and comfortable in winter by layering their clothes. The space between the layers traps air and prevents heat loss. Layers also let you move more freely than one bulky garment. And you can always take off a layer if you get too hot.

Properly dressed, you can stand temperatures down to zero. Below zero there is the danger of frostbite. If you have frostbite, your skin looks white or blotchy-blue and you cannot feel anything.

The fastest way to warm up a frostbitten area is to place it in warm—not hot—water. If this isn't possible, gently rub the frostbite with your hand or hold it against a part of your body that is still warm. But be sure you see a doctor as soon as possible. Frostbite can sometimes do permanent damage.

Some of the happiest holidays of the year come during the winter. The holidays probably began as a way to lift people's spirits during the harsh winter months. Also, since it was hard to work outdoors in the winter, there was more time for parties.

The ancient Roman feast of Saturnalia honored Saturn, the god of agriculture, in December. The Saturnalia was a joyous, one-week celebration when the Romans exchanged gifts, danced in the streets, and held masked balls. Masters and slaves changed roles for those few days.

No matter where you live, you find people celebrating the winter holidays with lights, gifts, and songs. Cities and towns sparkle with candles and decorations in December. Bright store windows hold shiny displays of toys and gifts. Many people decorate their homes.

In December, when days are short and the dark nights are long, comes Hanukkah, the Jewish festival of light. The holiday honors a special event in Jewish history. The Syrians had taken over the temple in Jerusalem and forbidden the Jews to worship there. When a group of Jews recaptured the temple, they rekindled the eternal flame that had always burned inside. Even though there was only enough oil in the lamp to burn for one day, the light miraculously burned for eight days. Jews around the world light eight candles during Hanukkah to celebrate the miracle.

In the early years of Christianity, the true date of Christ's birth was unknown. Then, in the year 350, Pope Julius I established December 25 as the official birth date of Jesus Christ. It is believed that he chose the date for a very good reason. Coming soon after the winter solstice, the date marks the start of spring's return and a rebirth of life on earth.

For Christians, Christmas became the most important winter holiday. Typical of the Christmas season are religious ceremonies, family parties, and the exchange of gifts.

Evergreen trees are an important part of Christmas. The reason is that these trees stay green all year long. They assure us that nature is still alive, even in the midst of winter. The custom of bringing trees into the house was probably taken from the Romans, who exchanged green branches for good luck. The Germans were probably the first to decorate the tree with stars, angels, nuts, and candies.

To entertain themselves on long winter nights, stargazers used to make up stories about groups of stars called constellations. One of the easiest constellations to spot in the winter sky is Orion, the Hunter. If you look toward the south, you'll see three

bright stars in a row. They form Orion's belt. Once you've found his belt, it's easy to make out the rest of the constellation.

You can also spot a good number of shooting stars during the winter. Many of these shooting stars are seen when earth crosses the path where a comet had passed. The shooting stars are part of the dust and debris left in space by the comet. Shooting stars are really big or small hunks of metal or rock that enter the earth's atmosphere at great speed.

If you are well protected from the bitter, cold weather, it is fun to ice skate, build a snowman, play hockey, or have a good snowball fight. While there's lots to do outdoors in winter, it is also the season to spend more time indoors.

By March the weather begins gradually to change. The cold winds fade away. The sun grows warmer. The days get longer. Green shoots poke up through the thawing ground. Buds begin to swell and burst open on the trees. The snow melts and streams begin to flow. Migrating birds return and hibernating animals come out of hiding.

Before you know it, winter is over. Spring arrives in all its glory.

Glossary

ARCTIC CIRCLE. An imaginary line drawn around the earth about 23 degrees south of the North Pole. It divides the Frigid Zone from the Temperate Zone. The Antarctic Circle is the imaginary boundary of the Frigid Zone that surrounds the South Pole.

AXIS. An imaginary rod that passes through the earth and connects the North and South Poles. The earth rotates, or turns, around its axis.

CHLOROPHYLL. The green substance in plants and tree leaves that produces food for the growing plant or tree.

DEMETER (dih-meet'-er). The Greek goddess of the earth and growing plants.

EQUATOR. An imaginary circle around the middle of the earth. The equator is the same distance from the North Pole and the South Pole.

EQUINOX. A term that means "equal night." Equinox refers to either of the two times in the year (about March 21 and September 22) when day and night are of equal length all over the earth.

ESTIVATE. To spend the entire summer asleep in one place.

FRIGID ZONE. The areas around the North and South Poles. It is always cold in the Frigid Zone.

HADES (hay'-deez). The Greek god of the underworld.

HIBERNATE. To sleep in one place for an entire winter.

LARVA. The stage in the development of an insect that comes after the egg hatches. The larva eats a great deal getting ready for the next stage, the pupa. A caterpillar is the larva of a butterfly.

MIGRATE. To move from one place to another. Certain birds, fish, and animals migrate every year at the same season and return at another season.

ORBIT. The path followed by earth as it moves around the sun.

PERSEPHONE (per-sef'-uh-nee). A Greek goddess, the daughter of Demeter.

PUPA. The stage in the development of an insect that comes after the larva stage. The pupa does not eat or move about. The mature insect appears in the next stage.

ROTATE. To turn or move around a center or axis. The earth rotates on its axis.

SATURNALIA (sat-ur-nail'-yuh). A joyful winter holiday celebrated in ancient Rome.

SEASON. A period of the year having particular temperature ranges, rainfall or snowfall, wind patterns, and so on. There are four seasons in a year.

SOLSTICE. The two times a year when the earth is tilted most toward the sun (about June 21) or most away from the sun (about December 21).

TEMPERATE ZONE. The part of the earth between the Tropic of Cancer and the Arctic Circle. In the Southern Hemisphere, the Temperate Zone is between the Tropic of Capricorn and the Antarctic Circle.

TROPICAL ZONE. The area around the equator where it is always warm. The tropical zone is bounded on the north by the Tropic of Cancer and on the south by the Tropic of Capricorn.

TROPIC OF CANCER. An imaginary line that circles the earth about 23 degrees north of the equator.

TROPIC OF CAPRICORN. An imaginary line that circles the earth about 23 degrees south of the equator.

ZEUS (zoos). The chief god of the ancient Greeks.

Index

About the Author

Melvin Berger is the author of over one hundred books. He was elected to membership in the New York Academy of Sciences in 1983, and has been awarded prizes by the National Science Teachers Association, National Council for the Social Studies, Child Study Association, and the New York Public Library. His books have been translated into fifteen languages, as well as prepared as filmstrips and audio tapes. Melvin Berger enjoys collecting antique microscopes and old scientific instruments, and lives in Great Neck, New York, with his wife Gilda.

About the Artist

Ron Jones was born and raised in Arizona. He has had numerous exhibits and won several prizes for his work, in addition to illustrating for books, magazines, and publications. He enjoys children, animals, gardening, spring, and summer, and especially appreciates "the charm and beauty that surround us in our everyday lives." Ron Jones is married, and his wife and their two children are also artists.